Where Are You Brother?

Written and Illustrated by: Taylor Darnell

ISBN: 0692544119
ISBN-13: 978-0692544112

DEDICATION

This book is dedicated to my brother, Rick.

You are forever by my side

I miss and love you brother.

IN MEMORY OF_____

THIS BOOK IS FOR_____
FROM_____

CONTENTS

ACKNOWLEDGMENTS

This book is for any child coping from a loss. Many experience different stages of grief filled with constant memories and feelings of loneliness without their loved one. The hardest stage is acceptance, acknowledging the loss. This book is to help kids understand acknowledging a loss does not mean their love ends.

This book is for all the children who need and want answers.

I still wake up somedays and forget my brother is no longer here on Earth, but I have come to terms that no matter what, he is always there, and our love will never go away. No matter the distance.

I want to thank my family and friends for continually pushing me to write this story.

Rick, my brother, your spirit has forever changed me.

THE LETTER

Hey brother, I'm writing you a letter,

I hope you get it soon;

My days have been so different here without you.

CONFUSION

Mom says you're somewhere beautiful.

Dad says it too;

But all I am wondering is... where are you?

MEMORIES

I'm going to start basketball

I hope you can see me play;

Remember the time you were running the wrong way?

WISH

Mom says you're up in the clouds.

Dad says especially when it shines;

I wish I could climb our tree and you could be all mine.

HOPE

Gosh, I miss you brother.

When I grow up I want to be just like you;

Someone others will look up to.

BELIEVE

Last night was so special.

I can't believe it's true;

I closed my eyes to dream and there I found you.

ACCEPTANCE

Before last night I feared you were gone.

But now I know;

You are always with me... you are everywhere I go.

LOVE

I hope you like my letter.

I can't wait to see you soon;

My Brother, I miss you, and I love you to the moon.

Where Are You Brother?

LOVE WILL NEVER END

ABOUT THE AUTHOR

Taylor Darnell
I was born April 24, 1992
I love the color Purple
I love animals
I have 2 sisters, Alex and Laylla
I have 2 brother, Rick and Liem
I have loved
I have lost
I have laughed
I have cried
My Hero is my mom
I love you.